DYNAMIC DELEGATION

DYNAMIC DELEGATION

A MANAGER'S GUIDE FOR ACTIVE EMPOWERMENT

Mark Towers

SkillPath Publications, Inc.
Mission, Kansas

Editor: Kelly Scanlon
Cover Design, Page Layout Design, and Illustrations: Wes Eastwood

ISBN: 1-878542-33-8

Printed in the United States of America

TABLE OF CONTENTS

TABLE OF EXERCISES

PREFACE

Delegation simply means "to entrust to another." Sounds simple, doesn't it? Yet most people never realize their potential in life because they never learn to delegate tasks and projects to others.

Quite simply, there are two key reasons for delegating:

1. There is too much work for one person to handle.
2. It is the best tool for empowering and "growing" people on your team. ("Growing" is helping people move up in the organization.)

However, delegating work is seldom easy. It involves trusting others. It means that a portion of a person's rewards and setbacks depends on someone else's ability to perform. This leads to fear of turning work over to someone else. But when people fear delegating, it restricts their growth. They tend to control things more closely—to guard their positions more tightly.

This hands-on, how-to, no-fluff, to-the-point handbook will get right to the heart of the matter, which is quite simply this: Delegation involves an internal struggle. The delegator must keep what he or she wants to give up—responsibility. Conversely, the delegator must give up what he or she wants to keep—authority.

Think, for a moment, of the three most successful people you know. More than likely, these people possess solid communication skills. Furthermore, they probably know how to work with others constructively. And they probably strive to accomplish some of their goals and objectives through others. Finally, they probably believe in making these folks feel good about doing the work.

Indeed, to some degree, your successful acquaintances have mastered the art of delegation. They are successful because delegating has allowed them to spend more time working on the things that are truly important to them.

You, too, can be like them. You've taken the first step by choosing to learn how to delegate. But please don't just adopt the information in this book—adapt it. Incorporate these concepts into your own style. Make them work for you in a genuine fashion. Over time, you will improve upon these concepts, teach them to others, and help others along their path of personal effectiveness.

Congratulations for taking the time to invest in and improve yourself. It's no secret that a lot of people just don't make the time to improve themselves. Woody Hayes, a great football coach at Ohio State University once said, "You're either getting better or getting worse." It's good to see that you've gotten serious about getting better.

Mark Towers

DELEGATION AND TIME

> ### *"Time—that is the stuff that life is made of."*
> — Ben Franklin

Not long ago, a young man sat next to a 72-year-old gentleman on an airplane. As they chatted, the older gentleman revealed that he was still a very successful businessman. The younger man asked him what made him successful and the older man obliged him. Then, near the end of the flight, the older man said: "The older I get, the quicker time seems to fly by. Enjoy life while you're young, son."

Later, the young man wondered how many times he'd heard someone say something similar during his life— forty, fifty, perhaps well over a hundred times? But for some reason, this particular incident finally compelled him to look up time *in the dictionary.*

The definition jumped off the pages at him. It read:
"Time is a nonspatial continuum in which events occur in an apparently irreversible succession from the past through the present to the future."

This definition seemed so concrete, so final, so powerful, so truthful. The words "in an apparently irreversible succession" drove home to him how irretrievable time is.

Once it's gone, it can't be called back. The definition gave him great insight into why time is so precious—insight he had never considered before.

Over the course of the next several days, the young man continued to think a great deal about time, tasks, and how he spent his time. Suddenly he came to the realization that, for the most part, time is a paradoxical human invention. On the one hand, it was invented to put structure, meaning, and purpose into people's lives. He realized that his own life was cued to calendars, clocks, and deadlines. Time had helped him achieve, measure, and predict. In that sense, time had helped him move from Point A to Point B. Time had helped him feed his family.

On the other hand, he deduced that time constraints can be dictatorial. They had caused him undue stress at times in his life. They had often kept him from stopping and enjoying himself.

He concluded that although the paradox of time would always exist, what he did with his time would determine his life. His challenge, he realized, was one of finding balance. So he made a commitment to himself and to his loved ones to live his life by these two simple, key principles:

1. *I have all the time I need to accomplish and finish the really important things I need to get done in life.*

2. *By completing these really important things, I will leave behind a very constructive legacy. My life will have been a meaningful one.*

He realized that the mission of his life was quite simply to maximize his potential. And it occurred to him that it was not possible to maximize his potential unless he committed himself to getting some things done through others.

What the young man concluded was that the ability to delegate effectively is the true challenge of time management in today's world. In other words, the young man had come to realize the *absolute necessity of delegation* in order to get things done.

> ### "It isn't easy to keep your mouth and your mind open at the same time."
> — Unknown

To begin the process of delegation, you must first know what it is that you want to accomplish. Then you must be able to break your goal or task down into manageable pieces by deciding what you can do and what *someone else* can do.

Here's an example. Suppose one of your wishes is to travel to Australia. These are the things you can do to achieve that goal:

- Save the money.
- Decide the approximate dates you would like to travel.
- Find someone who wants to go with you (assuming you don't wish to vacation alone).

These are some things you could effectively delegate to someone else:

- Call a travel agent and have information regarding flight schedules, best places to visit, tour packages, and so forth sent to you.
- Ask a neighbor to keep an eye on your house.
- Ask the post office to hold your mail.
- Ask the newspaper to hold your paper.
- Call the police and ask them to keep an eye on your house because you'll be gone for quite awhile.

Now, try Exercise 1. The purpose of the exercise is threefold:

1. To get you to think in long-term patterns.
2. To point out the importance of planning.
3. To enable you to break your plans into what you need to do personally and what you need to delegate.

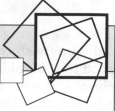

EXERCISE #1: BREAKING YOUR GOALS INTO MANAGEABLE STEPS

Consider the continuum below to be a representation of your life. On the line, place an "X" at the point you feel you are right now in life. For instance, if you feel you are one-third of the way through your life, place an "X" one-third of the way along the line. If you feel you are two-thirds of the way through your life, place an "X" two-thirds of the way along the line.

Birth———————————————Death

Next, examine your "X" in relation to the rest of your life. Think of at least two major things (wishes) you would like to accomplish. Then, in the space below, break those wishes into manageable pieces.
Consider:
1. What will I have to do to make that wish become a reality?
2. What activities can I delegate to someone else to make that wish become a reality?

What I can do:

_____
_____
_____
_____

What someone else can do:

_____
_____
_____
_____

There's a saying that goes something like this: "A goal is a dream (wish) with a deadline." The chances are very good that breaking your wishes down into bite-size chunks was not an easy one for you to do. Most people who complete this exercise report that they feel like they are leaving out critical steps.

This is a perfectly normal feeling—planning can never be perfect. Obviously, other details may crop up as you plan. You'll discover things "along the path" as time transpires, but remember that success begins with a "rubber-meets-the-road" plan.

The simple skill of breaking things down into what we need to do ourselves and what we need to delegate is seldom taught. In our culture, planning is something that many people don't like to do. Planning, they say, robs them of their spontaneity and creativity.

Yet most people who accomplish great things know how to plan. They know what to do themselves—and they know what to delegate.

But, as simple as it may sound in theory, delegation is an extremely hard skill to master (even when there are plenty of people to delegate to). It is one skill that very, very few people ever execute well—if at all. In fact, most people get fed up after a few delegations fizzle. They throw up their hands and say, "It's hopeless." They don't persist. They simply go back to doing the work themselves. Indeed, most people have been raised in families and work environments that instill the notion that if you want something done right, then you need to do it yourself.

As a result, people often jump into a project feet first, without considering any other viable options. Plunging fearlessly onward, they finish the project, feel a sense of accomplishment, and begin looking around for the next thing to do.

But consider Yvette, an excellent supervisor, who tells her people to stop and think each week about their work loads. She says, "Whenever you are doing work that could have been done by others, you are being overpaid." She encourages those she supervises to plan each week by considering the four major resources they have to work with: manpower (woman power), method, machines, and materials.

Yvette stresses that people need to think first about how they can effectively use the skills, resources, and energies of others in order to get work done. When she appraises people, she coaches them on their ability to delegate to others. She wants to make sure that everyone in the organization has a chance to grow. Her favorite saying is: "If you want to move up in this organization, train your people to replace you!" Now, that's a line that will motivate people to become better delegators.

> *"A mistake is evidence that somebody has tried to accomplish something."*
> — John Babcock

> *"A good spectator also creates."*
> — Swiss Proverb

The Drop, Delay, Delegate and Do Model offers an effective way to approach your tasks, your projects, and your time.

Assume you are getting ready to plan and prioritize your day. The first question you would ask is *"What can I drop?"* In today's busy world, it is important to think about which tasks you can eliminate. You simply need to decide which tasks give you the highest payoff and which ones give you little or no payoff. Prepare yourself for the fact that you simply must say no to some things. This is what is called setting *posteriorities*—these are things that you decide not to do. But be forewarned: It's easier to identify top priorities than it is to identify low priorities!

Ask yourself, or others for that matter, these questions:

- What report or task can I not do?
- What can I (or must I) quit doing in order to use my time better?

If you are a perfectionist, consider the words of the management guru Peter Drucker: "It is more important to be effective than efficient."

After determining what you can drop, ask *"What can be delayed?"* Since you can realistically do only one thing at a time, you must decide what you can put off. Mark Twain jokingly said, "Don't put off until tomorrow what you can put off until the day after tomorrow."

In fact, Twain's remark contains some wisdom for today's managers. Delaying items of non-urgency, items of non-importance, and items of medium-range importance is a key and necessary tactic in today's working environment. Being able to delay tasks and keep track of them is characteristic of someone who can multitask effectively. Here's a case in point:

One assistant manager reports that he keeps a yellow "OBE file" in his right hand desk drawer. He explains: "Those three letters stand for 'overcome by events.' Whenever one of my supervisors gives me something I think is of fairly low priority, I put it in that file. I periodically review this file. I find that approximately 90 percent of what I put in that file I never end up doing!"

Now that's called creative procrastination! The manager successfully delays some tasks until they are overcome by events. Then, of course, they are *dropped off* of everyone's agenda. Consider adopting the manager's philosophy. Keep a yellow OBE folder in your desk drawer. Why yellow? Yellow is the color of optimism. Hope and optimistically forecast that many of the things you drop in this folder will be overcome by events. It is an easy, fun, and practical way to approach time management.

The third step gets to the real heart of the matter. The question you must ask yourself is *"What can be delegated?"* The ability to delegate well and redistribute work to others determines two things:

1. Your overall worth to any organization.
2. Your overall accomplishments in life.

At this point, you may be thinking: "I can drop things and I can delay things, but I don't have anybody to delegate to!" Indeed, many organizations have downsized. They have become "lean and mean." Many people report that finding someone to delegate tasks to is no easy chore.

Effective offices must operate with an overall sense of reciprocity or teamwork, with the attitude of "you help me, and I'll help you. We'll get the work done and then go home."

The fourth and final question is *"What can I do?"* Concentrate on the most urgent and important items— the high-payoff items, the really important things that true achievers make time for. These become the projects and the tasks you will be remembered for.

The Drop, Delay, Delegate, and Do Model

- **What can I drop?**
- **What can I delay?**
- **What can I delegate?**
- **What can I do?**

"If I could, I would stand on a busy corner, hat in hand, and beg people to throw me all their hours."

– Bernard Berenson

"Everything degenerates into work."
– Peter Drucker

Think about the number of things you delegate each day without even thinking about it. For example, you may delegate the well-being of your children to child care centers or schools. You may pay others to prepare your meals in a restaurant. If you commute, you pay others to transport you from one destination to another. Indeed, society is filled with specialists who allow you to leverage your time better.

Why, then, don't more people learn to delegate effectively at work? Many people go about their jobs completing low-priority tasks that are of little or no consequence in comparison to the big picture. The high-priority tasks often succumb to the low-priority tasks that get an "urgent" label attached to them.

The ability to delegate effectively is a power tool in the tool chest of successful people. They realize the importance of attaching and completing these high-priority tasks. They know that lower priority tasks must be assigned to others. Successful people know and understand the importance of delegating; unsuccessful people struggle with the concept throughout their lives.

Here are some key reasons people struggle with the concept of delegation. Do you see yourself in any of the situations?

Creatures of habit. Some people simply become creatures of habit and overlook the opportunity to delegate. They get so caught up in the pace of what they are doing that they don't stop to ask themselves, "Could I get someone else to do this?" Ask yourself that question both at home and at work. Remember the old adage: "When I let go, you grow." Furthermore, people grow by concentrating on other tasks and goals that have a higher payoff.

Of course, it sometimes costs money to have other people perform services. However, time is of far greater value than money. Time is a finite resource and money is not. Once time is gone, it is gone forever. When monetary resources are depleted, individuals can always make more money. This mind-set is the mind-set of successful people.

Sign of weakness. Many people feel that delegating tasks is a sign of weakness. Self-sufficiency or the "Lone Ranger" mentality is a sign of strength to many people. These people feel that passing work off to others is a sign of ineptitude, lack of strength, the inability to organize, or the inability to see things through to their conclusion.

Perhaps one hundred years ago being totally self-sufficient was a sign of strength. But in today's information age, ignoring the opportunity to delegate is ignoring an incredibly valuable tool.

Perfectionistic tendencies. Some people have perfectionistic and controlling tendencies. These people fear that others will not do a task or activity as perfectly as they would have. Sometimes this condition is referred to as the "paralysis of analysis."

Perfectionism and overcontrolling can be crippling because it often forces people to spend their time on low-payoff tasks rather than on high-payoff tasks.

Effective delegation is a great deal like effective planning. Initially, delegation and planning call for substantial investments of time. Just as it takes time to do sound planning, it takes time to teach, explain, and delegate things to others. However, delegation pays vast dividends in the long run.

Self-gratification. Some people enjoy doing some of the tasks themselves. They like routines, busy work, and their established "comfort zones." They enjoy doing the nitty-gritty, day-to-day, bump-and-grind tasks because it often gives them an opportunity to ignore the higher payoff tasks. This subtle form of self-sabotage actually keeps some people in their psychological comfort zones for their entire lives.

Consider Cindy, a salesperson who was promoted to sales manager. After her promotion, she continued to call on her clients and perform some of the same routines that went along with her previous job title. Cindy ignored her new managerial tasks and spent a good deal of time doing her busy work, making her comfortable sales calls, and pursuing other activities she was used to performing as a salesperson.

Administrative problems began to appear as Cindy continued to spend her days in her typical salesperson mode. By refusing to delegate some of her enjoyable tasks and concentrate on the new administrative, supervisory chores, Cindy sabotaged herself, lost her new supervisory role, and ended up quitting her job.

Takes too much time. Some people may argue, "It takes longer to explain and delegate this job than it does for me to go ahead and do it myself." Think about that attitude. First, it ensures that when the task (or something similar to it) arises again, the person is destined to do it again. Second, it indicates a lack of leadership—the person is unwilling to invite his or her associates to grow and develop. Third, it signifies a weak manager whose mind-set is governed more by completing urgent tasks (putting out fires) than those that have long-range importance.

The late Paul "Bear" Bryant was one of the most successful football coaches of all time. Moreover, he was regarded as a true leader. The men who coached under Bryant reported that he allowed them to coach; they felt that he had faith in their ability to carry out and execute vital things that needed to get done. There were many tasks that Bryant could have handled himself, but he delegated them instead. By doing so, he reaped great rewards—including several national football championships.

Fear of being disliked. Some people fear they will be disliked for piling more work on others. Obviously, leaders must be tuned in to the work loads of others. Communication among team members is critical. Most people love interesting and challenging work. They would rather work for a skillful delegator than one who is afraid to challenge or entrust them.

Consider the following ad that appeared in *The Times* of London in the early part of this century. It read: "Men wanted for hazardous journey. Low wages, bitter cold, long hours of complete darkness. Safe return doubtful. Honor and recognition in the event of success."

This ad was placed by Ernest Shackleton. He was looking for a tough crew that he could take on his journey to discover the South Pole. The morning after the ad appeared, over 5,000 men were waiting outside *The Times'* offices. Shackleton reached the South Pole in 1907.

The lesson of this story is that people want to be challenged to do great things. An effective delegator has an obligation to help individuals exceed the expectations they have of themselves. In turn, the organization will push beyond simple survival and on to surpassing its own expectations.

Scott Peck, one of the great psychotherapists of our times, once said, "Most people want to live lazy lives." This statement is relevant to the concept of delegation. Truly great leaders are great delegators, but not because they want to pawn their "To Do" list items on to others.

They realize that their contribution and their ultimate impact are long-range in nature. They are the complete opposite of lazy! They are simply dedicated enough to think things through, to make several things come together and happen simultaneously, and to positively impact the environments in which they live and work.

> ### *"Do what you can, with what you have, where you are."*
> – Theodore Roosevelt

Think about the tasks you do each day. If you are performing tasks that you know you could delegate to someone else in your office, note them in the space below.

Next, using the information in this section of the book, identify your reasons for not delegating those tasks.

Finally, think of ways to overcome those obstacles so that you begin delegating those tasks—and at the same time empower yourself and others.

Tasks I Should Be Delegating	Reasons I Don't Delegate Them	How I Can Overcome Those Obstacles

CREATING A CLIMATE FOR EFFECTIVE DELEGATION

"Leadership is example."
– Albert Schweitzer

*"Nobody can be exactly like me.
Sometimes even I have
trouble doing it."*
– Tallulah Bankhead

More often than not, when people are asked to write down words to describe their situation at work, they choose words such as these:

Hectic	Fast-paced
Chaotic	Firefighting
Panic	Overwhelming
Crazy	Stressful

Indeed, many people do often live and work at a frenetic pace—so much so that some people describe today's working atmosphere as "permanent white water."

The challenge of managers in today's organizations is to create an office environment that hums. An effective climate for encouraging delegation and maximum productivity is one of *subdued urgency*. Subdued urgency can best be defined as being 90 percent thoughtful and well-planned and only 10 percent panic, firefighting, or craziness. (Face it–there will always be an element of change, shifting priorities, and fire-fighting.) Subdued urgency can only be accomplished through open and honest communication between all people in the office.

Consider Jerry, who manages an office in the not-for-profit arena. It is a fast-paced, no-frills office with mountains of paperwork to process. No one earns a very high salary—including Jerry. But Jerry has developed high-powered, loyal, and high-producing people in his office by following what he calls the "Platinum Rule of Delegation":

> **"Never delegate anything to anybody that you wouldn't be willing to do yourself—including making the coffee."**

Jerry swears by this rule, noting that the days of "Do it because I am the boss and I said so!" are gone forever. He believes that people need to be treated as equals. Furthermore, he realizes that modeling the behavior he expects from his people is absolutely critical. He stresses, "I never *tell* anybody to do anything—I always *ask*."

Linda, one of Jerry's staff people who handles many of his delegated tasks, has worked for him for nearly five years. She says: "Jerry works just as hard as the rest of us. He never acts superior to us. He treats us with respect. This place does get hectic at times. There are some days that we can't even take a lunch break. But we seem to get through it all."

Other people in Jerry's office also sing his praises. They feel that Jerry has helped them grow as professionals. They feel that he is one of them, and they actually look forward to the tasks Jerry delegates to them.

Finally, Jerry says: "People don't want to be managed; they want to be lead. That means they don't want to be controlled or handled. I used to be an authoritarian person and looked to dump everything I could on people. It took me a number of years to understand that this is not how people want to be treated."

Today, Jerry takes time to think things through, to communicate thoroughly with employees, and to delegate effectively. He knows that he must delegate effectively if he expects himself and the other employees not only to survive—but to thrive.

Appropriately, Jerry keeps a plaque on his wall that reads:

> **"Aim for success, not perfection.
> Never give up your right to be wrong,
> because then you will lose the ability to learn
> new things and move forward with your life.**
>
> **Remember that fear always lurks behind
> perfectionism. Confronting your fears and
> allowing yourself the right to be human can,
> paradoxically, make you a far happier
> and more productive person."**
>
> —Dr. David M. Burns

It's delightful to walk into a busy office such as Jerry's where employees seem to be enjoying themselves in spite of the heavy work load. Like bees around a hive, employees seem to have a sense of vision, mission, and passion. It's invigorating to be around people who simply love what they are doing. This type of nurturing office environment can best be described as a "win-win" environment.

There are, however, "lose-lose" working environments. In a lose-lose office, people do tasks grudgingly. They look to dump work off on one another and see who can do the least amount of work.

Then there are "win-lose" environments. This type of environment is generally characterized by "perceived" winners (people with power) who dump, not delegate, work to "perceived" losers (people with little or no power).

Creating and maintaining a win-win type of office takes genuine commitment from the leaders. For a leader to effectively create a win-win office environment, he or she must possess these key attributes:

- A positive mental attitude
- A strong work ethic
- A sense of fairness
- A willingness to empower others
- The ability to give praise and gentle criticism
- The ability to have fun
- The ability to pitch in and help when deadlines are tight and when people are "under the gun to get it done"

"The brighter you are, the more you have to learn."
– Don Herold

EXERCISE #3: FINDING WAYS TO IMPROVE YOUR WORK ENVIRONMENT

Step 1: Jot down three words that describe your office/working environment.

_____

_____

_____

Step 2: Ask other people in your office to write three words that describe the working environment. Have everyone keep their words secret—don't share them with one another.

Step 3: Call a meeting to discuss everyone's choice of words. Ask your co-workers and supervisor to honestly share their feelings about the office work processes.

Set the ground rules for the meeting by reading this statement aloud:

"We can communicate with people on four different levels.

On Level 1, we can tell people what they want to hear. This a superficial level.

At Level 2, we can tell people what we think. This is the deeper level of communication that we encourage today.

When we communicate on Level 3, we can tell people what we feel. It is perfectly fine to express your feelings at this level today.

On Level 4, we can share our gut feelings.

If you have deep feelings regarding an issue, please feel free to express them. In other words, let's consider this a safe haven for honest and open communication today."

Step 4: Begin the meeting. Have people share the three words they wrote down, and have someone take notes.

Step 5: Have a brainstorming session. Throw out wild and crazy ideas (and not-so-wild and crazy ideas) that would help create a sense of subdued urgency, teamwork, and the ability to effectively delegate tasks to one another.

Step 6: Get consensus on at least three ways that the team can create this sense of subdued urgency in the working environment.

Step 7: Post these agreed-upon concepts in the office for all to see.

Step 8: Follow up two weeks later to assess how things are going. If necessary, have another meeting to fine-tune the office environment.

Step 9: Ask someone to be in charge of "mid-course correction" of the office environment and these types of meetings. In other words, at any time, a person in the office can ask this individual to have another brief meeting in relation to any of the previous meetings.

One final note: Two key items will help you keep these types of meetings running smoothly:

1. Plan the meetings around lunch or provide snacks. Remember this pearl of wisdom—"If you feed them, they will come!"
2. Encourage people to have a sense of humor—to laugh at their circumstances and working relationships.

When someone says, "You're as silly as a goose," say thanks for the compliment. These rowdy, independent animals have created a natural work team that allows them to delegate responsibility and authority to one another in a most productive fashion. It truly is a thing of beauty to watch and study. Their natural ability to model the win-win environment is something human beings need to thank them for.

Here are several observations that wildlife experts have made about geese. Notice how the actions of the geese in flight provide a model for effective delegation.

OBSERVATIONS	LESSONS
Observation #1: As each goose flutters its wings, it creates an updraft for the bird following it in the V-formation of migration. By flying in this V-formation, the geese are able to migrate 72 percent further than if each bird flew unaccompanied.	**Life's Lesson #1:** People who share a common vision and sense of common direction can get further faster by supporting one another.
Observation #2: When the lead goose tires, it peels off the point position and rotates back into the V-formation. Another goose then steps up and takes its turn fighting into the wind from the point position.	**Life's Lesson #2:** It pays to take turns. By delegating critical tasks to all team members, everyone in an organization can grow.
Observation #3: The lead goose (on the point) never honks. The geese behind the leader continue to honk praise and encouragement to the lead goose.	**Life's Lesson #3:** The power of praise and recognition is critical to success as people delegate significant projects to one another in an organization.
Observation #4: Sometimes two or three geese break away from the formation in order to look for a better wind current or a more creative and better way to fly.	**Life's Lesson #4:** An effective organization believes in the "culture of celebrated discontent." It constantly experiments with new ways of being. Successful organizations often forget quickly and learn slowly. In today's environment, constant improvement through teamwork is an absolute necessity.
Observation #5: When a goose gets sick or wounded and has to go down to land, two other geese fall out of the formation and go with it to support and protect it. They stay with it until it dies—or is able to return to the formation. Then the "escort" geese try to catch up with their own flock or another formation of geese.	**Life's Lesson #5:** When tasks are tough, people need to support one another. Delegation and teamwork require follow-up, dialogue, and support.

The next time you see a flock of geese flying overhead in a V-formation, stop, observe, and think about all the formations (teams) of which you are a member.
Remember that it's OK to be as "silly as a goose."

"What gets rewarded gets done!" is a saying that rings true. Another saying that seems to make sense is "Everyone listens to his or her favorite radio station all day long. It's WIIFM, or What's In It For Me." To be a successful delegator, you must remember these two short bits of philosophy.

Indeed, these two basic, philosophic, and bottom-line approaches to the world can be disputed. Motivation is a tricky and complex issue. Many people argue that motivation is such a deep, internal phenomenon that it is extremely difficult to comprehend or define. In fact, Peter Drucker once said, "We know nothing about motivation. All we can do is write books about it."

Poor delegators do a lot of *telling*. Successful managers do a lot of *selling*. Delegating work to be done involves some salesmanship or persuasion by the delegator—particularly on the front end of the task to be assigned. It means taking the time to explain the importance and magnitude of the task to the delegatee so that the delegatee can share the vision of the completed task. This shared vision is the essence of teamwork—of the win-win philosophy.

The task of the effective delegator is not to psycho-analyze or find fault with people. It is to observe people and dialogue with people concerning their basic needs. Understanding that different people respond to different motivators makes the process of delegation much easier to "sell" to the appropriate delegatee.

Use Exercise 4 to examine different motivators and how they can be useful in terms of getting work done through others.

EXERCISE #4: WHAT MOTIVATES ME?

Rank the following ten items according to the degree they motivate you to get things done in the workplace. For instance, if time off (more leisure time) is the thing that you crave the most, put a 1 in front of it. If personal growth experiences are the second most important motivators for you, then rank that item number 2. If job security is number 3, give it a 3—and so on down the list. Use a pencil, take your time, and examine yourself as you rank the items.

_____ Job security

_____ Pitching in and helping others after getting my own tasks completed

_____ Fun (interacting with others, laughing, and enjoying others on the job)

_____ Prizes (tangible things I can earn that are not monetary rewards)

_____ Personal growth experience (going to a seminar or learning more about a computer, etc.)

_____ Advancement (more autonomy or perhaps more power within the organization)

_____ Free food (I like to eat and enjoy fellowship with my co-workers.)

_____ Time off work (more leisure time away from work)

_____ Recognition (I like it when people consistently recognize my contributions—either verbally or in writing)

_____ Money/profit-sharing/bonuses

Now that you have completed this exercise, you have some insight into what your "carrots," or positive motivators are.

Now consider these ten items and their importance to all people. Use the items as a checklist for observing and eventually talking with people about the key reasons they come to work in the first place.

Don't use the list as a tool for finding fault or performing psychoanalysis. It is simply a tool for creating more teamwork, dialogue, and a win-win environment within the workplace.

One final word of caution: People are, of course, dynamic and ever-changing. They are not static. Things that they viewed as positive motivators for themselves last year may not be this year. The effective delegator, then, is much like the effective parent. He or she realizes that children's needs change as they grow, just as the needs of adults do.

"The teacher is like the candle which lights others in consuming itself."
– Ruffini

During the past several years, much research has been done on the role of humor, play, and laughter on the job. Many researchers, trainers, and people in the field have emphasized that humor, play, and laughter during the workday can enhance productivity, creativity, and enthusiasm among employees.

In fact, some researchers have stated that workers who make work upbeat and fun are almost twice as productive as workers who do not. Knowing this, of course, gives you a tremendous advantage as you delegate work.

Two workers from Pennsylvania, Jim and LaDonna, claim that humor is the ultimate power tool in their workplace. They say it was no secret that their company was downsizing and that everyone was feeling extremely uneasy. Both Jim and LaDonna felt that they could lose their jobs too.

But they realized that the same work load still existed. The same amount of paperwork still had to be done in spite of the downsizing. As a result, everyone shared equally in handling the work load. Everyone was delegated the same amount of work—including Jim and LaDonna.

Jim and LaDonna decided to take action to keep the morale up—to make work as fun and as upbeat as possible. Here are some strategies they use to make work fun while they get their jobs done:

- Put cartoons on the company bulletin board
- Give a mini-workshop on laughter, play, and humor
- Keep a camera handy in order to capture the times when someone makes a mistake or does something silly

- Hold a raffle once each quarter for meals or desserts that nearby restaurants donate
- Once each quarter before work, conduct a half-hour seminar on cooperative games that can be played in the workplace
- Bought some humorous cassette tapes and encouraged employees to check them out for their commutes to and from work

Jim and LaDonna say that implementing these ideas has brought people in their department closer together and relieved tension and stress as well. But they remind others who might consider these ideas to be mindful of what is appropriate in their offices and to be tasteful with their use of humor and play. They also caution that humor and playfulness can be overdone.

What are some things that you could institute in your workplace to create more harmonious working relationships among the people on your team?

Write your thoughts in the space below.

_____

_____

_____

_____

_____

_____

_____

_____

_____

_____

Now choose one of your ideas and plan what you need to do to implement it.

_____

_____

_____

_____

_____

_____

_____

_____

_____

Recently, several people in a seminar were talking about the concept of delegation, about getting work done and accomplishing their goals. They were complaining about the fact that they had too much work to do, not enough time to do it in, and not enough human resources to handle their current work loads. These seminar participants were looking to one another for answers to their situations.

An engineer in the room raised his hand and said: "When we have discussions or disagreements like this in our engineering firm, we have a brainstorming session. One of us writes the four 'M's' on a flip chart or a blank sheet of paper—manpower, method, machines, and materials. We know that these are the only four categories of resources in the entire universe. We know that if we brainstorm long enough around these four springboard words, we'll find a way to become more productive."

Several people attending the seminar liked this suggestion and wrote it down. But another gentleman raised his hand and said: "I am an assistant pastor in a small church. I have limited manpower—including volunteers from the congregation. I'm not looking for any better methods. I don't need any more computers or machines. I'd like some new materials for the church, but I know we can't afford them. I do have some staff people and some volunteers I can delegate things to, but they never seem to do the job correctly—at least not as well as I could. Most of the time I just do jobs myself because that seems to take less time. I really need help at managing my time better. Does anyone have any suggestions for me?"

There was a long pause. Then a large man with a ten-gallon cowboy hat, cowboy boots, and a face that had been chiseled by the Texas wind spoke slowly and said: "I used to never delegate anything—even though I had plenty of people to delegate to. But nine years ago, a fellow gave me some invaluable advice regarding life, success, and delegation. Now I take the time to delegate everything I possibly can. And if I don't have the time to delegate effectively, I make the time! You see, this friend who gave me the advice is a self-made multimillionaire. He is a man I respect and admire a great deal."

He continued, "My friend, Jerry, told me that success in life is much like a cattle drive. Each steer in the herd represents a project or task. There are a lot of these tasks, and they head in all different directions. But Jerry said that it is impossible and even unimportant that every steer in the herd be heading 00.90 latitude. It's just important that the herd be headin' in the general direction of west!"

This man had created a visual picture for everyone in the room, and everyone laughed in unison. But his story contained real wisdom. In a few short sentences, he had pinpointed three vital aspects about success:

1. *Busy people are not perfectionists.* Successful people cannot oversupervise every steer in the herd. The same can be said about oversupervising every project or task that gets delegated. The successful person keeps pushing things forward, realizing that some projects won't need much nudging. Yet, some will need much more attention.

2. *Delegatees (members of the herd) must be given tasks to complete.* This is where the risk factor comes into play. Turning things over to others is risky—just as a cattle drive may be risky and dangerous at times. Yet, taking this risk is truly imperative. Today, there is just too much to handle individually. In other words, avoid the "Lone Ranger" mentality.

3. *A successful person moves in the proper direction with a sense of vision and some established goals—* just like a cattle drive would proceed on its mission—headin' west. At times, the herd may plod and move slowly, but persistence pays off in the long run.

Remember this visual image of the cattle drive. Use it as a metaphor for getting things done and for achieving your potential. Make a concerted effort to push all projects ahead—even if it's just a bit at a time. Furthermore, make a concerted effort to delegate more work to talented people who can effectively get things done.

> ***"We're all here for a short while. Get all the good laughs you can."***
> – Will Rogers

THE NUTS AND BOLTS OF DELEGATION

> *"The great aim of education is not knowledge but action."*
> – Herbert Spencer

> *"Living is entirely too time-consuming."*
> – Irene Peter

Clearly, delegation works best when it is a two-way, interactive process. People will not commit very readily to something they don't fully comprehend. It's now time to examine the nuts and bolts of delegation in order to more effectively understand it and, more importantly, to execute it correctly. This "how-to" section will enable you to pass tasks on to others with the least amount of risk.

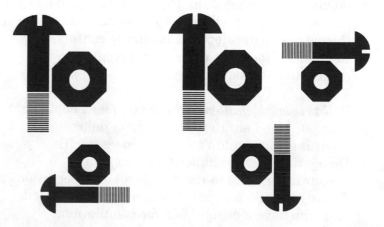

"People have one thing in common: they are all different."
– Robert Zend

At least 70 percent of effective delegation involves selecting the right individual to handle the delegated tasks. Here are five questions to ask yourself when choosing that person:

1. *Is this the person "furthest down" in the organization who can handle this task successfully?* Always attempt to "grow" people—that is, empower them—at the lowest possible level within the organization—particularly during these days of "flattening the pyramid" (making organizations more flat and flexible) and creating effective work teams.

2. *What is in this project for the delegatee?* Enlist the delegatee's support by "selling" that person on the benefits of completing the project. But the benefits must match the delegatee's expectations; if the delegatee doesn't view them as benefits, you have the wrong person. Benefits may be additional monetary compensation, the opportunity to develop new skills, the possibility of job advancement, or the chance to develop new company contacts. Remember, too, that praise and recognition are critical to successful delegation.

3. *Will this work challenge the delegatee?* People hate being dumped on. Remember, don't delegate anything you wouldn't want to do yourself. Delegation means challenging people and encouraging them to rise to a level of expectation. Above all, pick delegatees who are goal-oriented and who have a compulsion for completion.

4. *Is this person someone who can effectively tolerate frustration?* Face it—delegating work to someone else means that person must be able to deal with anything that may go awry on a project. The person you choose must feel comfortable asking questions of you, the delegator, as well as of other people who can help achieve the project's goals, meet its deadlines, and rise to its challenges.

5. *Is this person trustworthy and communicative?* A good delegator and a good delegatee must be able to level with each other. Honest communication is critical. In fact, one successful delegator tells each of his delegatees: "Don't tell me what you think I want to hear about this project. Don't tell me what you think about this project. Don't tell me what you feel about this project. But tell me your 'gut' feeling about this project." In other words, choose someone who will not patronize you. As the delegator, you must model "give-it-to-me-straight honesty" and expect the same from the delegatee for the partnership to be effective.

Keep this list of questions handy. Refer to it often as you delegate tasks to others. Refer to it now as you complete Exercise #6.

"When the student is ready, the teacher will appear."
– Confucius

You are a sales manager for a television station. Your sales force has been doing extremely well. In fact, the general manager of the station plans to hire one new salesperson. Your job has been to supervise the staff of four (soon to be five) salespeople and help them sell more advertising.

You have done an outstanding job supervising your staff during the past three years—and you've been servicing some of the larger accounts yourself. In fact, you've chosen not to delegate these accounts to any of your salespeople because you originally sold the television time, and you feel your relationship with these critical clients is extremely important. Losing any one of these accounts would cause the station serious financial damage. You fear your other salespeople would not be able to handle these accounts as well as you handle them.

But now your position has grown to the point that you must juggle many administrative projects as well as sales-oriented issues. Most of these administrative tasks involve non-sales-related items that are causing you to work longer hours each week. Your supervisor insists that you delegate some of your work load to your salespeople. The two of you brainstorm some options. Here is what you come up with:

Option 1
Delegate at least one of your major accounts to one of your better salespeople. Train that person to eventually service your customer.

Option 2

Delegate some of your daily administrative duties to one of your salespeople. These are duties that need to be repeated weekly. Negotiate some form of compensation or "trade-off" with the salesperson.

Option 3

Delegate your daily administrative duties to all of your salespeople (including the new person coming on board) and allow them to function as a self-managed team. Let them handle these tasks as they see fit. Ask them to recommend a compensation agreement to you and to the general manager of the station.

Option 4

Continue the status quo for a while. You and your supervisor can play "wait and see" for another three months or so. You're getting paid good money—more than anyone else in your department—so you can work the extra hours. You know that your existing customers and your administrative tasks are of critical importance. Bite the bullet. Tell your supervisor that you can handle the situation and that eventually you will have it all under control.

Choose the best option from those presented or provide one of your own. Explain your selection. Then compare your answer to the explanations on the next page.

_____

_____

_____

_____

_____

_____

_____

_____

ANSWER KEY TO EXERCISE 6

Option 1 is not the best option. Getting and keeping customers is the reason your station is in business. Servicing the customer is the highest priority—no matter what your position in the company. If you are the best person to service the account, then you should do so. Besides, staying involved in sales keeps you sharp and focused; it lets you know what your salespeople are faced with day in and day out. It helps you maintain your creative edge and gives you an opportunity to show the sales staff that you lead by example.

Option 2 is not the best option. It is true that tasks that must be repeated daily or weekly are real "time robbers." These tasks are the most easily delegated. But why delegate all the mundane or "junk" tasks to just one person? Doing so could lead to the burnout of an effective salesperson.

☆ **Option 3** is the best option of those provided. This option allows you to entrust your sales staff with tasks that need to be done. It will build more teamwork within the organization, more effectively flatten the pyramid by giving people a say about their department, and create more dialogue among the people who work together on a daily basis. It magnifies the philosophy, "None of us is as smart as all of us."

Option 4 is not the best option. No one should want to live a workaholic, unbalanced life. Unfortunately, many people never step back from the big picture, examine their work load, and delegate effectively. They just can't "see the forest for the trees."

Option 5 (your option) is the best option. If you chose an option of your own, compare it to the explanations provided here. Decide whether you still think it is the best alternative.

_____

_____

_____

_____

_____

_____

_____

_____

_____

_____

"The surest way for an executive to kill himself is to refuse to learn how, and when, and to whom to delegate work."
– J.C. Penney

As you analyze your work day, think about the tasks that only you can do. In fact, one effective delegator sets an alarm to go off every half hour to remind her to stop and analyze what she's been doing during the past thirty minutes. She asks herself, "Is this something only I can do or is it something I can delegate to someone else?"

Here are some tasks you can delegate to free up more time for the things that *only you can do*:

Delegate routines. It has often been said that people are creatures of habit. Think of the habitual things people do on a daily basis. They habituate; that is, they stay within their "comfort zones" and never really grow or change much.

Now think about how you could better delegate some of your day-to-day routines to others. For instance, do you spend part of each day making copies, sending and receiving faxes, typing, and involved in other tasks that you could delegate?

Delegate areas of your job that require technical expertise. Are you responsible for handling spreadsheets, the company phone system, a records retention schedule, or a computerized inventory system, for example? If you are the only person in your office who can perform these tasks, you will be forever saddled with them. Technology will only continue to explode. Begin now to teach other team members about these areas.

Delegate the tasks and projects that are the most unfamiliar to you. There's no sense taking twice as long to complete a task someone else could do better or in half the time. Let someone else handle projects they are accustomed to handling. Doing so will benefit both you and the person to whom you delegate the task. If you need to be apprised of the nuts and bolts of the project, schedule time for this after the project has been completed or at specific intervals as the project is completed.

Delegate the functions of your job that you enjoy least. If you dislike detail work such as working on the budget, find someone who enjoys those types of things. Provide support and training, but allow the delegatee to handle the entire task. Then, have that person apprise you of the details after completing the endeavor.

Delegate some enjoyable things to others. Remember, hoarding all the pleasurable tasks can be detrimental to morale. Sharing the good with the bad says a lot about your character and overall leadership ability.

Delegate tasks or challenges that will interrupt the routine of those who have boring jobs. People need the challenge of change to keep them fresh, creative, and happy.

Delegate time to people so they can cross-train one another on their day-to-day tasks. Cross-training enhances quality, teamwork, and morale within an organization. It also makes it easier for workers to cover for one another when someone is sick or absent or transfers to another position.

Delegate projects involving the critical, visible issues of quality, quantity, cost, and timeliness to self-managed or self-directed teams. Quality, quantity, cost, and timeliness are the only four variables that can be measured in the workplace. As time goes by, more managers are being asked to give up some of their power in those areas to teams. These teams will accept the challenge and approach a project with new insight, spread the work out evenly, and give everyone input into the work processes.

When you turn these critical projects over to teams, you must become more of a facilitator, coach, advisor, and educator, which is a positive role to have in the fast-paced information age.

Managers used to be paid to practice **POSDIC**:

Plan

Organize

Staff

Direct

Inspect

Control

But now managers are being looked upon to delegate POSDIC skills to others who work in teams.

The bottom line: Take the time to be a teacher. Then go learn more skills and continue teaching them. By repeating the learning-teaching-learning-teaching cycle, you will make yourself more valuable to your organization. You will become a true team player who leads within an ever-changing, growing, and dynamic organization.

Finally, consider the process of giving away or delegating tasks as being similar to giving away meaningful gifts to others. Treat the tasks you delegate as precious treasures. Don't view delegation as "dumping stuff" on others. See it as an opportunity for creating synergy between two people. See it as an opportunity for mutually benefiting all involved. See it simply as a win-win situation.

This commitment to individual and team excellence conveys to delegatees that you are serious about producing quality work. Furthermore, it conveys the overall notion that "none of us is as smart as all of us." That could also be termed effective leadership.
On the other hand, there are some tasks that you should never delegate. As Harry Truman would say, "The buck stops here." There are some jobs you should take full responsibility for and complete yourself. Use Exercise #7 to consider tasks that you would never consider delegating.

Exercise #7: Identifying What Not to Delegate

Make a list of three things you are currently doing on your job that you would never consider delegating to anyone else.

1. _____

2. _____

3. _____

Why wouldn't you delegate these tasks?

_____

_____

_____

_____

_____

Now compare your response in Exercise #7 to the following list of items that should never be delegated—except as a last resort. If you must delegate these items, make sure that you do so carefully and articulately.

Never delegate the task of long-range planning. Planning involves vision and your long-range stake in the organization. Delegating this task is like delegating your future to someone else.

Never delegate the task of selecting key players to your team. It is permissible to delegate some of the paperwork in the hiring process, but don't delegate the final selection. Would the management of a professional basketball team or baseball team delegate its selection of players to someone else? Obviously not.

Don't delegate the task of monitoring the team's key project or key function. Simply remember this word—*accountability.* The person responsible for a project, task, or a key set of results should keep a finger on the pulse of the project. Also remember this old management axiom: "People respect what you inspect, so inspect what you expect."

Frank, an office manager, once delegated one of his most vital functions (he considered it too mundane and routine) to one of his assistants. His assistant made several clerical errors. Once these errors were discovered, Frank was reprimanded by his supervisor's supervisor. Later, the organization used this event as an example of how not to do things.

Don't delegate the task of motivating fellow team members. The *leader's* leadership is required in certain situations. The leader must be a person who is looked up to because he or she takes the time to "pump up" the key players. People don't care how much a leader knows unless they know how much the leader cares. Taking the time to motivate team members shows your genuine commitment to them.

Don't delegate evaluating fellow team members. Appraisal is never an easy issue—that's why many people put it off and often avoid it altogether. The number one characteristic of an effective "people person" is honesty.

So, grab the "bull by the horns" and evaluate people openly and honestly. They may not always like what they hear, but they expect and want honesty.

Don't delegate the opportunity to reward team members. Team members want to be appraised by their leader. Make the time, take the time, and give people their "day in the sun."

Don't delegate rituals. A leader's attendance is always a plus at key community and organizational functions. Attend funerals, graduations, ground-breaking ceremonies, and celebrations. Successful people suit up and show up!

Don't delegate "touchy" or personal matters or crises. Items of this nature also require personal attention. When you delegate these types of items, you may end up being scapegoated for a situation that goes awry.

Don't delegate items that help set precedents or create future policy. Pioneering is critical in this day and age. Harry Truman once said, "Gather your information, make your decision, and tell your critics to go to hell!"

Obviously, Truman was intimating that at times we all get paid to make tough decisions. Do not delegate anything that shows a lack of decisiveness. There is an old saying that goes: "Make a decision and then make it right." Sometimes a leader must do exactly that.

It has been said that communication is about power and that power is about limits. This, of course, implies that boundary-setting means saying no to some things. Indeed, there are some things we must say no to; there are some things that you must avoid delegating.

Because delegation always involves communication, effective delegators know how to set their limits (or boundaries). They know what to handle themselves.

EXERCISE #8: REEVALUATING WHAT YOU DELEGATE

Now that you have read the information about what tasks not to delegate, reexamine the items you listed in Exercise #7. Are there other tasks or projects you should consider not delegating? If so, list them in the space below.

_____

_____

_____

_____

_____

When is the best time of day to delegate? Highly successful time managers possess great insight into the patterns and overall timing of their personal body clocks and their personal "prime times." They know their "internal prime times" and they know the "external prime times" of their workplace.

What is your "internal prime time"? Know when to spend time alone so that you can make appointments with yourself to plan. Know when to find time to think ahead. Realize that one hour of uninterrupted quiet, internal prime time is worth three-and-a-half hours of fast-paced, phone-ringing highly interrupted time.

In fact, it is most often during this uninterrupted time that successful time managers effectively plan the tasks and projects they are going to delegate to others. Taking this time to plan is much like "sharpening a saw."

The analogy here is a simple one: People who chop wood must stop to sharpen their saws periodically. When the blade gets dull, a wood chopper's efforts are not nearly as effective. When wood is chopped with a dull blade, the wood chopper is simply working harder—not smarter. The same holds true for planning tasks and delegations during internal prime times. This planning time or "saw sharpening time-out" enables you to work smarter and not harder.

Furthermore, as an effective time manager, you must also understand the "external" patterns of your personal body clock and the external patterns of your workplace. In other words, you must know the best times to make phone calls, hold meetings, talk to customers face to face, and engage in other activities that involve interaction with other people.

Some highly effective time managers have made the following observations about the work-a-day world:

■ Most people in North America are "morning people." They feel most productive, alive, and awake before noon.

■ The timing of tasks is extremely critical. Research shows, for example, that there are less incidents of surgical problems when surgery is performed before noon. In fact, there are 20 percent more problems with surgery that is scheduled after noon. Research also shows there are fewer quality control problems with automobiles built on Wednesdays in Detroit. Monday is the day when most quality control problems occur.

■ One time management consultant actually stresses that the best time to have a highly productive meeting is at 10:00 o'clock on Tuesday morning because it's not too close to noon and by that time of morning, people have already had time to go to their work stations. Furthermore, Tuesday is in the middle of the week, when people are more into the swing of things.

■ During the last half hour of any shift or work day, effective people should be communicating with themselves and others about the next shift in order to get the maximum productivity from themselves and others.

The best time, then, to delegate work to others is during the last hour of any work shift. When you plan your delegations for the end of the day, you don't waste vital "prime time" at the beginning of the day or shift. You are also implying to the delegatee: "Here's the task, make it happen, fit it into your schedule, come find me if you run into any snags or obstacles or if you have any questions."

You are, in effect, empowering the delegatee to think about how to personally "make the task happen."

> ### *"We should all be concerned about the future because we will have to spend the rest of our lives there."*
> – Charles F. Kettering

EXERCISE #9: PLANNING END-OF-DAY ACTIVITIES

Besides holding delegation conferences and arranging the next shift's priorities during the last hour of the workday, think of some other tasks you feel are best handled during the last hour of your workday. Write them down here and begin working them into your daily schedule.

_____

_____

_____

_____

_____

_____

_____

_____

_____

_____

_____

_____

_____

A delegation conference is the setting in which the delegator hands off the work to the delegatee. The communication between the two parties during this conference is absolutely critical.

The following things must be in place in order to have an effective delegation conference:

- A quiet area
- Sufficient time to communicate
- Solid preplanning by the delegator
- A visual reference guide

In fact, these conditions are much like the conditions necessary for being an effective teacher.

The overall approach of teacher (delegator) to student (delegatee) is an excellent mind-set with which to approach the delegation process. However, never consider the delegatee as your subordinate. Avoid at all costs the attitude of "I am better or higher ranking than you." Such an attitude inhibits teamwork, sound communication and, perhaps most importantly, the delegatee's growth.

How do you create each of the conditions necessary for holding an effective delegation conference? Consider these suggestions:

Find a quiet area. Today's work environments can be quite hectic. Phones are ringing, printers and fax machines are buzzing, and people are conversing. Yet many people still choose to delegate standing up in the hallway—or perhaps by dropping by someone's desk to delegate a task at the last conceivable minute.

Don't delegate "on the fly." Find a quiet area. Reserve an empty conference room. Ask to use an unoccupied office or cubicle. If all else fails, go to a nearby restaurant to find a quality "quiet" spot. Delegating from a quiet area shows a genuine commitment to quality communication.

Allow sufficient time to communicate. Remember this rule of thumb: "Ninety-five percent thoughtfulness is better than 105 percent panic." Delegation conferences are often rushed. There is often no time for sufficient dialogue, questions, and quality communication. When you plan your delegation conferences, schedule in a "fudge factor"—an extra amount of time for asking questions and for providing further clarification. Then, if the conference ends early, everybody wins.

Indeed, excellent teachers always seem to know how much material they can cover in a class period. Their timing is superb! The delegation conference is no different—you must budget the time to explain the project and then create a fudge factor or safety net of time for answering questions.

Solid preplanning by the delegator. Effective delegators always have a game plan. They know that proper planning always leads to proper execution. To be an effective delegator, you must do your homework and have your act together. A delegation conference is not the time to fly by the "seat of your pants."

In fact, it is during the planning stage that you should ask yourself:

- What task or project am I delegating? What do I want the end results to be?

- Who should do this job? Why am I selecting this person?

- What motivates this individual?

- How much authority will this individual need?
- How much supervision will this person need?
- What checkpoints and mini-deadlines should I set up to ensure that this project is going properly?

A visual reference guide. According to experts, 70-75 percent of all learning is visual. An effective delegator draws pictures and provides visual reinforcement as needed. If you take the time to sketch the necessary elements of the project or task, you will put the delegatee at ease.

Furthermore, taking the time to offer visual aids will probably exceed the expectations of the delegatee and set the stage for a strong relationship. Most delegation conferences are typified by a supervisor delivering instructions in a monotone "do-this-because-I-said-so" voice.

Use the form that follows to help you set the stage for an effective delegation conference. This delegation planner is designed to help both you and the delegatee focus on the task at hand. It will remind you to find a quiet place, schedule enough time to communicate properly, and concentrate on solid, focused preplanning.

Delegation Planner

The Finished Project:_____

To Be Completed By:_____
                                            (person)

Projected Deadline:_____

Checkpoints/Milestones:_____

Notes/Reminders/Unique Items:

_____

_____

_____

_____

Authority Level:_____

(Levels of Authority—Boundary Setting)
1. Gather the facts. I'll decide.
2. Recommend pros and cons. I'll decide.
3. Recommend a decision. I'll approve it.
4. Handle the project, but let's talk and agree on certain aspects of it before it begins.
5. Take any necessary action, but inform me as to what happens.
6. Take care of the project. There's no need to get back to me.

"Never learn to do anything: if you don't learn, you'll always find someone else to do it for you."

—Mark Twain

Power is not a negative concept. Many people view power as a corrupting, evil, and negative force. But, in fact, to be an effective delegator, you must view power as the ability to positively impact your relationships. As the delegator, you must view the delegation process as a compliment to the delegatee.

Although you must positively influence, maintain, and nurture a relationship in your role as delegator, you are also responsible for defining the delegation, communicating clearly, and setting boundaries for the delegatee.

Explaining and defining limits is particularly vital to the process of delegation. Consider the following six levels of boundary-setting that can be utilized during the delegation conference.

Boundary #1: The delegator says to the delegatee: "Examine the situation thoroughly. Bring me all the data you possibly can. I'll make the final decision."

This boundary works well when you have asked someone to do some research. The delegator is not letting go of much power. He or she wants the delegatee to do some investigative work and that's all. But the delegator must make clear that the investigative work and research is important—not trivial.

This boundary could also be utilized to train inexperienced people or to familiarize people with an area with which they are unfamiliar.

Boundary #2: The delegator says to the delegatee: "Pinpoint the problem. Make a list of possible plans of action. Examine the pros and cons of each option. Then recommend a course of action. I'll make the final decision."

This boundary can be used to create bonding, discussion, and dialogue between the delegator and the delegatee. It gives both parties a chance to explore one another's styles. Again, the delegator is retaining much of the power at this level of delegation.

Boundary #3: The delegator says to the delegatee: "Investigate the task and make a decision about the best course of action to take. Discuss the task with me, but don't do anything until we've agreed upon our course of action."

A delegator who uses this method entrusts the delegatee's investigative abilities and value judgments. Obviously, this boundary implies that the delegator has gained quite a bit of confidence in the delegatee.

Boundary #4: The delegator says to the delegatee: "I want you to handle this project. But before you take any action, let's talk to one another. I want you to handle this your way, but I want to give you some input before you begin."

This boundary implies a high level of trust between the delegator and the delegatee and the establishment of a highly productive relationship. Furthermore, it implies that the delegator is intuitive enough to begin grooming people to take over his or her position. Remember, people get promoted by training others about their own jobs.

Boundary #5: The delegator says to the delegatee: "Go forward with this project. Complete it. Then come and tell me how it turned out."

This boundary indicates that the delegator has empowered the delegatee to make decisions. It implies a high degree of friendship or bonding with another individual. Fast-paced and very small businesses often operate at this very high level of empowerment, communication, and trust.

Furthermore, by asking the delegatee to provide feedback, the delegator keeps himself or herself in the loop of communication.

Boundary #6: The delegator says to the delegatee: "Go ahead and handle the situation. There's no need for you to tell me what you did."

In effect, the boundary has been erased! Achieving this level may take years of people working together, camaraderie, and familiarity with one another's work processes and habits. In fact, this level of delegation and teamwork can be observed in good, solid marriages.

The degree of authority that you grant to a delegatee depends on many factors, including:

- The complexity of the task.
- The deadline.
- The importance of the task.
- The expertise of the delegatee.
- The confidence that the delegator has in the delegatee.

Unfortunately, many people continually delegate to the same people all the time. Furthermore, they never risk delegating above the fourth level to anyone. Effective delegators scrutinize their patterns of delegation to find out where they can improve.

Effective delegators come to realize that each level of authority (boundary) requires a different investment of their time. Moreover, more contact between delegator and delegatee is required at lower levels of delegation. Many effective individuals have found that increasing what they delegate does not necessarily mean finding more discretionary time—at least not at first. Logically, delegation must eventually occur at the fifth or sixth level in order for the delegator to recover large amounts of time.

These six boundaries are designed to empower both the delegator and the delegatee. When delegating tasks and working with people on a daily basis, take some time to think about the following key guidelines before setting boundaries. Thinking about these items will give you a strong insight into your delegation style and into the overall process of setting boundaries.

Have I . . . ?

❏ Thought and planned the delegation well?

❏ Clarified in my mind the desired end result of the delegation?

❏ Selected the right individual?

❏ Set the appropriate controls, checks, or milestones?

❏ Established an upbeat and motivational environment for this delegation to occur?

❏ Communicated to the delegatee that he or she will be accountable for the task or project?

Get started now on setting the boundaries for the tasks you delegate by completing Exercise #10.

For which of the tasks that you delegate would each of the following boundaries be appropriate? List those tasks under the appropriate boundary category below.

Boundary #1

_____
_____
_____
_____

Boundary #4

_____
_____
_____
_____

Boundary #2

_____
_____
_____
_____

Boundary #5

_____
_____
_____
_____

Boundary #3

_____
_____
_____
_____

Boundary #6

_____
_____
_____
_____

After reading this section, do you feel you need to change the boundaries of any tasks that you routinely delegate? If so, list those tasks here and note the new boundary you should consider.

_____
_____
_____
_____
_____
_____

"The world is full of willing people;
some willing to work, the rest willing
to let them."
—Robert Frost

Assume that you've had an effective delegation conference. The delegatee understands the boundaries and the assignment, leaves the conference, goes to work on the project, and then gets stuck.

If the problem that crops up is out of the prescribed boundaries that you and the delegatee have agreed upon, then the delegatee must, in fact, contact you. The subsequent conversation or meeting that you have with the delegatee is what is called the "teaching moment." During this moment, both you and the delegatee need to discuss what occurred outside of the boundary that needs further clarification.

On the other hand, the delegatee may say, "I'm stuck. We have a problem!" But after hearing the problem, you realize it should have been handled by the delegatee. It is within the boundaries the two of you agreed upon.

Quite simply, by establishing the boundary level that you did, you wanted the delegatee to take the time, energy, and resources to solve the problem. After all, this is what delegation is about—"When I let go, you grow!" During the teaching moment in this particular situation, an effective delegator will notice some critical things about the delegatee and why he or she is "putting the monkey back on the delegator's back." This, of course, is reverse delegation.

Here are some of the key causes of reverse delegation:

The delegator doesn't explain things well enough during the delegation conference. Ray, an effective delegator, says that when something doesn't go quite as well as expected during the delegation process, he looks at the delegatee and says, "Didn't I explain that well enough?"

This question is powerful. It means that as the delegator, Ray is willing to accept part of the responsibility for missed communication and, in turn, a nonacceptable performance. By asking this genuine question and inviting a genuine response, Ray exudes participative leadership. He truly sees himself and the delegatee as partners.

The delegatee is fearful of risks or lacks confidence. Some people are more confident than others. To build confidence in the delegatee, catch the person doing something right and reinforce it. Use oral and written praise. And remember, offer criticism to empower and to teach—not to evaluate or to "put people in their place."

The delegatee feels there is a lack of adequate information to do the job. During the delegation conference, it is the delegator's job to provide the delegatee with the appropriate information to do the job. A delegator who doesn't provide the necessary information may have to spend valuable time later either explaining the project again or reclaiming responsibility for all or certain parts of it.

The delegatee does not have the proper resources to do the job. Many times, the resources to complete a project may be in short supply or hard to locate. At this juncture, the effective delegator encourages the delegatee to be creative by using a concept called "Completed Staff Work."

This concept was invented by Napoleon Bonaparte. When he commanded his army, a lower-ranking officer would come to him and say: "Sir, we have a problem. The supply lines have been cut." Napoleon would reply: "I've got enough problems. Please bring me some solutions."

A successful manager once suggested that all people in positions of leadership need to post these seven letters outside of their office doors: DBMPBMS. They stand for "Don't Bring Me Problems. Bring Me Solutions." This manager has adapted Napoleon's idea for modern times. She expects delegatees to use their powers of creativity to overcome obstacles resulting from resource shortages.

The delegator sends double messages. Some delegators send conflicting signals. On the one hand, this type of delegator tells the delegatee to act independently. On the other hand, the delegator truly has a need for control.

Although it is often difficult for the delegator to recognize this type of behavior, the delegatees pick up on it very quickly. When a delegatee points out this need for control to the delegator, the delegator often denies it. The fallout here is of the worst kind: The delegatee feels stifled and either quits or asks to be transferred. Then the delegator has the project back on his or her desk.

Remember, people do not want to be managed or supervised—they want to be led. Since effective leaders are effective delegators, they must bear in mind that reverse delegation can and will occur. The key to success is to identify reverse delegation and to handle it immediately.

THE SURE-FIRE METHOD OF DELEGATION (ETFP x 2)

"It's a funny thing about life; if you refuse to accept anything but the best, you very often get it."

—Somerset Maugham

To help you remember the steps involved in the delegation process, remember this simple formula: ETFP x 2. This formula captures the eight essential components of an effective delegation.

What does ETFP stand for?

Easy-to-Follow Procedures.

Here's how the ETFP formula will help you remember the eight ingredients needed for successful delegation:

E = Entrust and Enlist
T = Teach and Touch
F = Familiarize and Follow-up
P = Praise the Process and Participate in Feedback

E = Entrust and Enlist

T = Teach and Touch

F = Familiarize and Follow-up

Px2 = Praise the Process and
Participate in Feedback

Entrust and enlist. Delegation involves *entrusting*
someone else—at least to some degree. To entrust to
someone else means that you simply must let go of
perfectionist tendencies. Entrusting work to others is
always a gamble. The delegatee may fail or let you
down. But it's a gamble that you must take in today's
fast-paced world.

If you take the time to find the right individual to
entrust your work to, you reduce the chances of failure.
Selecting the right individual is a major portion of
completing any delegation properly.

In addition to entrusting the delegatee, you must *enlist*
that person's support. That does not mean selling the
delegatee on a notion or idea. It means gaining that
person's partnership. It means taking the time to
explain the project. It means getting the delegatee to
"buy into" the project for self-advancement as well as
for the advancement of the organization—a cause of
which you both are a part.

Practice the concept of *enlistment* by communicating to
the delegatee (either verbally or nonverbally) these
three things:

■ This is a critical task that must be done—it's not just
busy work.

■ I would never delegate anything that I'm not willing to do myself.

■ Say, "I need your help"—and say it sincerely.

Teach and touch. As a delegator, you must remember the importance of *teaching*. Use these three "T's" to guide you through the teaching phase of the delegation process:

Time. Agree on an exact deadline. ASAP is too vague. Use exact time estimates.

Tools. Bring the necessary tools to the table in order for the delegatee to work effectively. If necessary, teach the delegatee how to properly use the tools.

Trouble. Teach the delegatee his or her boundaries. Describe what kind of trouble to anticipate as the work progresses. Teach the delegatee to communicate with you when trouble occurs or when a situation arises outside the boundaries that you established. Remember, nobody wants the whole ship to sink.

The second half of the "T" portion of the formula involves the concept of *touch*. Your job as a delegator is to touch people, or to empower them to feel a greater sense of accomplishment. Carl Rogers, the great psychotherapist, once said, "We all need to be touched—both literally and figuratively."

When delegating work to someone else, remember to figuratively touch that person with your eyes. Good, solid eye communication signals dedication, compassion, and seriousness.

Familiarize and follow up. Working together involves partnering. To work together successfully, partners must be *familiar* with each others' work processes, work loads, and personalities. Take the time to *familiarize* yourself with the work load, demands, and idiosyncrasies of the person you delegate to. Share compassion for the delegatee's current work situation or work load. Create dialogue. If you show an interest in your delegatee's situation, he or she may reciprocate by finishing the delegated tasks in an efficient and timely manner.

The second half of the "F" portion of the formula reminds the delegator to *follow up* on the project or task. An old delegation axiom is, "People respect what you inspect so inspect what you expect." Use this tongue twister as a reminder of how important it is to follow up and take a look at the work the delegatee is doing. During follow-up sessions, give the delegatee an opportunity to present his or her work. Doing so will instill the delegatee with pride and dedication. One note of caution: Remember that some delegatees are so competent they don't need their work inspected. If you've established this boundary level with the delegatee, don't hover. If you do, you risk alienating that person.

Praise the process and participate in feedback. *Praising the process* means taking the time to recognize and appreciate the very fact that you and another person are attempting to work together effectively and efficiently. It also means praising any noteworthy aspect of any delegation—no matter how successful or unsuccessful the delegation as a whole was.

Again, remember that delegating work to others involves risk. Many times, the delegatee will complete the project, but not necessarily the way you would have done it. Praising the process means thanking the delegatee and pinpointing the things he or she did well—no matter how small or insignificant.

Of course, all good delegators will teach the delegatee how to correct the things that did not go well. But this should occur subsequent to specific, genuine, and immediate praise. In fact, Sandy, a woman working in Georgia, said that after each delegated project, her supervisor makes a list of all of the things he feels could have gone better as well as a list of what he thinks went well during the delegation.

Immediately after the project is completed, he praises the entire delegation process and the growth, effort, and attitude of Sandy and any other employees involved.

Then he files his notes until the next delegation opportunity presents itself. At that time, he pulls out his corrective feedback list and uses it as a teaching tool to ensure that the next delegation goes even more smoothly.

Sandy revealed that her supervisor was being promoted rapidly in the organization—and rightfully so. Here is a man who understands the power of praise. Furthermore, he knows how to empower, coach, and use corrective feedback to "grow" his people.

The second half of the "P," *participate in feedback*, actually refers to giving the delegate a voice in the delegation process. Today's organizations are becoming more flat and flexible; that is, the traditional and hierarchical pyramid chain-of-command seems to be gradually flattening in many organizations.

In light of this phenomenon, employees (delegatees) in many organizations are being asked to give feedback to their supervisors (delegators). This is a healthy concept! People should be given the opportunity to appraise one another.

As a delegator, grant delegatees an opportunity to rate you, even if your organization does not require you to do so. Receiving feedback will provide you with valuable input into your style of communication. Feedback will help you to change, to grow, to shift paradigms, to challenge traditional assumptions, to become more creative, and to become an even more effective delegator.

Effective delegators ask three simple questions of the people they delegate to:

1. What do I do that really helps you when I delegate tasks or projects to you?
2. What do I do that impedes the process of delegation?
3. What can I do to become a better delegator?

So, there you have it: ETFP x 2—eight Easy-to-Follow Procedures for delegating effectively.

TESTING YOUR DELEGATION READINESS

Now complete the following quiz, which is a self-examination and readiness checklist. Answer the questions by placing a "T" for true or an "F" for false in the blank before each statement.

_____1. Delegation is a skill that is relatively easy to master.

_____2. People delegate many things without even thinking about them. In other words, delegation is really a key part of living in today's service-oriented world.

_____3. Effective delegators could be called "lazy." They often give the work on their "To Do" lists to others because they don't want to do it themselves.

_____4. Effective delegators ask people to take on tasks for them—they don't order them to do so.

_____5. Geese in flight provide a good model for delegating to one another within a team setting.

_____6. There are some things that are so important that it may be best not to delegate them—or at least to take great care in delegating them.

_____ 7. Effective delegators are so good at persuasion that they don't need to inform delegatees of the rewards or payoffs they'll receive for handling the delegated tasks.

_____ 8. Delegation and teamwork occur more readily in an upbeat and positive work setting—not in a stiff and formal setting.

_____ 9. Selecting the right person is the most critical aspect of a successful delegation.

_____ 10. It is unnecessary to analyze the tasks that can be delegated to others. Delegation should happen spontaneously.

_____ 11. It is best to hold delegation conferences first thing in the morning.

_____ 12. When delegating, it is important to match the delegatee's level of authority with the level of responsibility. This can be done by setting boundaries.

_____ 13. Reverse delegation is always a result of the delegatee having inadequate skills or a lack of motivation to do the job.

_____ 14. Delegation can be broken down into a simple, understandable process.

See the next two pages to check on your delegation readiness.

ANSWERS TO DELEGATION READINESS QUIZ

1. *False*. Delegation is difficult to master. Most people have a hard time letting go of their tasks.

2. *True*. Delegation is critical in our everyday living. We delegate the care of our teeth to the dentist and our children to child care, for example. In fact, "outsourcing" work, or delegating it to other firms or people, has become a key strategy in today's fast-paced work environments.

3. *False*. Effective delegators lead by example. They handle their share of the load and spread tasks to others in order to get more things done.

4. *True*. No one likes to be told what to do. In fact, "I need your help with this" can be music to the ears of some people.

5. *True*. Honk. Honk. Honk. Remember mother nature's example as you create teamwork through delegating back and forth to one another.

6. *True*. Some tasks are like glass—drop them and they will break. Take care as you "juggle glass balls." Take even greater care if you delegate the juggling of these glass balls to someone else.

7. *False*. Remember this: What gets rewarded, gets done. Look for things that motivate people. Find out their "hot buttons" and reward appropriately.

8. *True*. Good working environments are characterized by flexibility and fun.

9. *True*. Selecting the right person is the most critical aspect of any delegation.

10. *False*. The delegator must first stop to consider only the tasks he or she can do, and then consider delegating other types of tasks.

11. *False.* It is better to hold delegation conferences near the end of the day.

12. *True*. Matching authority with responsibility is a key factor for getting work done through others.

13. *False*. Since delegation requires ongoing communication between the delegator and delegatee, reverse delegation can result from a lack of clear communication by either party.

14. *True*. Delegation is a simple process; however, few people master it.

Congratulations!

Now that you have read this book and completed the exercises in it, you're on the way to empowering yourself and others to get things done through dynamic delegation.

BIBLIOGRAPHY

Belasco, James, and Ralph Stayer. *Flight of the Buffalo: Soaring to Excellence, Learning to Let Employees Lead.* New York: Warner Books, 1993.

Buchanan, W. T. *The Motivating Manager.* Wimberly, TX: Value Concepts, 1988.

Buchholz, Steve, and Thomas Roth. *Creating the High-Performance Team.* New York: John Riley & Sons, 1987.

Covey, Stephen. *The Seven Habits of Highly Effective People.* New York: Simon & Schuster, 1990.

Douglass, Merrill E. and Donna N. *Time Management for Teams.* New York: American Management Association, 1992.

Hill, Napoleon. *Think and Grow Rich.* New York: Fawcett-Crest Books, 1960.

Mackay, Harvey. *Beware the Naked Man Who Offers You His Shirt.* New York: William Morrow & Company, 1990.

Maddux, Robert B. *Delegating for Results.* Los Altos, CA: Crisp Publications, 1990.

McCay, James T. *The Management of Time.* Englewood Cliffs, N.J.: Prentice-Hall, 1959.

Weber, Eric. *The Indispensable Employee.* New York: Berkly, 1991.

Winget, Larry. *The Ya Gotta's for Success.* Tulsa, OK: Win Seminars, 1991.

Select from these SkillPath Books for Your Professional and Personal Growth

To order any of these resources, or to request a complete SkillPath BookStore catalog, call toll-free **1-800-873-7545** or **1-913-677-3200**.